Sri Daya Mata and Sri Mrinalini Mata are two of the foremost disciples of Paramahansa Yogananda (1893 – 1952), founder of Self-Realization Fellowship/Yogoda Satsanga Society of India and world-renowned author of *Autobiography of a Yogi*. He personally trained both of them to carry on his worldwide work after his passing.

Sri Daya Mata served as president and spiritual head of SRF/YSS for more than fifty years, from 1955 until her passing in 2010. She was succeeded by Sri Mrinalini Mata, who currently serves in that position.

SRI MRINALINI MATA

President and spiritual head of
Self-Realization Fellowship/Yogoda Satsanga Society of India

Visiting the Saints of India With Sri Daya Mata

by Sri Mrinalini Mata

With excerpts from letters by Sri Daya Mata

Self-Realization Fellowship
FOUNDED 1920
Paramahansa Yogananda

ABOUT THIS BOOK: The material in *Visiting the Saints of India With Sri Daya Mata* was originally published by Self-Realization Fellowship in its quarterly magazine, *Self-Realization,* which was founded by Paramahansa Yogananda in 1925.

First Edition, 2017.

Authorized by the International Publications Council of
SELF-REALIZATION FELLOWSHIP
3880 San Rafael Avenue
Los Angeles, California 90065-3219

ISBN-13: 978-0-87612-797-1
ISBN-10: 0-87612-797-9

Printed in the United States of America
1253-J5127

Table of Contents

Yogoda Satsanga
Society of India

CELEBRATING 100 YEARS · 1917-2017

INTRODUCTION

In this book Sri Mrinalini Mata, president and *sanghamata* of Self-Realization Fellowship/Yogoda Satsanga Society of India, recounts her experiences of traveling with Sri Daya Mata during a trip to India from July 1961 through January 1962. Originally recorded during a talk to monastics at the SRF International Headquarters in Los Angeles shortly after her return, her reminiscences were later published in serial form in *Self-Realization* magazine. As 2017 marks the centennial of Paramahansa Yogananda's work in India, it is a fitting occasion to bring out this inspiring account for the first time in book form.

Though Daya Mata had made an earlier extended trip to India in 1958–59, this was Mrinalini Mata's first visit. Her experiences in India were truly remarkable, for she not only came in contact with two of India's most revered twentieth-century saints — Sri Anandamoyi Ma and Sri Sitaramdas Omkarnath — but she also was night and day in the presence of Daya Mata, who today is widely revered as a saint herself. With her own deep spiritual understanding and receptivity, which unfolded during her years as a close personal disciple of Paramahansa Yogananda — one of the preeminent spiritual masters of modern times — Mrinalini Mata was exceptionally suited to perceive and narrate the profound spiritual experiences that took place in the company of these divine souls. Also, during her years of living in the "inner circle" of Kriya Yogis who followed Paramahansaji, Mrinalini Mata had the good fortune of company with a number of true saints of God-realization in the Guru's ashrams in America, including his highly advanced disciples Rajarsi Janakananda, Sri Gyanamata, and others. She brings all of this background to the insightful and inspiring narrative presented in this book.

The trip was also recorded photographically. Sri Ananda Mata, sister of Sri Daya Mata,* took many of the photos shown in these pages, and others were taken by Mrinalini Mata herself.

---

* Daya Mata (1914–2010) and Ananda Mata (1915–2005) were among the earliest disciples of Paramahansa Yogananda in the West. They joined the Self-Realization Fellowship monastic order at a young age and were among the small circle of the Guru's closest disciples — serving him and his work unstintingly for more than seventy years. Daya Mata was president of SRF/YSS for fifty-five years until her passing and Ananda Mata was a member of the SRF/YSS Board of Directors for many decades.

Even before she made this pilgrimage, Sri Mrinalini Mata had imbibed a deep reverence for India and her saints from her guru, Paramahansaji. She first met him in 1945, at the Self-Realization Fellowship Temple in San Diego, when she was only fourteen years old. Just a few months later, her desire to dedicate her life to seeking and serving God found fulfillment when, with her parents' permission, she entered Paramahansaji's ashram in Encinitas, California, as a nun of the Self-Realization Order. He personally bestowed on her the final vows of *sannyas* in 1947, after she had been in the ashram only about a year; and he chose for her the name "Mrinalini," which refers to the lotus flower, traditionally regarded in India as a symbol of purity and spiritual unfoldment.

Through day-to-day association during the years until the time of his passing in 1952, Paramahansaji devoted much personal attention to the spiritual training of this young nun. Sri Daya Mata wrote: "Gurudeva made clear to all of us the role for which he was preparing [Mrinalini Mata], giving her personal instruction in every aspect of his teachings and in his wishes for the preparation and presentation of his writings and talks." She would later become editor-in-chief of Self-Realization Fellowship's publications. Through deep attunement with the Guru and her own tireless efforts, Mrinalini Mata has been instrumental in the editing and publication of many of Paramahansa Yogananda's major literary works.*

Though this small volume focuses mainly on Mrinalini Mata's inspiring encounters with the saints of India, the primary purpose of that 1961 trip was to continue the work begun by Daya Mata and Ananda Mata during their previous visit in 1958–59 — building and strengthening the Yogoda Satsanga Society organization that Paramahansa Yogananda had begun many years earlier but which had severely declined in the decades of his absence in America. To this end, Daya Mata, Ananda Mata, and Mrinalini Mata spent many weeks at the YSS Ashram in Ranchi, mentioned only briefly on pages 62 – 64.

Subsequent to her first trip, Sri Mrinalini Mata made several more visits to

---

* Among the works that have been published as a result of her efforts are Paramahansa Yogananda's masterful commentary on the four Gospels (entitled *The Second Coming of Christ: The Resurrection of the Christ Within You*), his critically acclaimed translation and commentary on the Bhagavad Gita (*God Talks With Arjuna*), several volumes of his poetry and inspirational writings, and three lengthy anthologies of his collected talks and essays.

India to help guide the work of Sri Yogananda's society there and to lecture on his teachings in principal cities of the subcontinent. As SRF's vice president, she assisted Sri Daya Mata for decades in overseeing the spiritual and humanitarian activities of SRF/YSS, including the worldwide dissemination of Paramahansa Yogananda's teachings; the establishment and guidance of temples, centers, and retreats; and the spiritual direction of the Self-Realization Fellowship monastic communities.

In 2011, shortly after the passing of Sri Daya Mata, Sri Mrinalini Mata was elected president and *sanghamata* of Self-Realization Fellowship/Yogoda Satsanga Society of India. In all she has dedicated more than seventy years to selflessly serving Paramahansa Yogananda's work.

In honoring the 100th anniversary of Yogoda Satsanga Society of India, which Paramahansa Yogananda founded in 1917, Sri Mrinalini Mata wrote:

> My heart rejoices as together we celebrate this auspicious centennial year commemorating the founding of our beloved Gurudeva Sri Sri Paramahansa Yogananda's Yogoda Satsanga Society of India....When I think of how

Guruji's Yogoda Satsanga Society has grown from a small "How-to-Live" school for boys in Dihika, to an organization encompassing large ashrams, a vibrant and growing monastic order, and more than two hundred meditation centers throughout India — as well as numerous educational institutions and charitable services — I feel his tremendous joy....

It was my privilege to accompany Daya Mataji on several of her trips to India. I cherished as she did the pure, sincere devotion to God, which is India's special heritage, reflected in the wonderful YSS devotees we met. Those visits and other later trips to Guruji's homeland are among my most treasured memories, engraved forever on my heart and mind.

— Self-Realization Fellowship

Visiting the Saints of India With Sri Daya Mata

"Where Ganges, woods,
Himalayan caves, and
men dream God —

I am hallowed; my body
touched that sod."

— Paramahansa Yogananda

CHAPTER 1
ARRIVING IN INDIA, OUR SPIRITUAL HOMELAND

India is not something you can describe in words; it is an experience. There is much there that may seem difficult if you look only on the outward surface. But the true essence of India is a spiritual experience. It is something that seeps into your being, almost without your knowing it, until suddenly you are fully in that magnetism, and you feel, "Oh, now I know why Gurudeva so much loved India! *This* is his India; *this* is the land that was able to produce a being like my beloved Guru."

Years ago when our blessed Master [Paramahansa Yogananda] was with us, sometimes in the evenings — especially in those early years in Encinitas when he was a little more free from organizational duties — he used to spend hours in the dining room or the drawing room with all of us gathered around him; and many of those happy times were spent talking about his beloved India. He told us about his early life there, but most of all what we enjoyed hearing from his lips were the stories about the divine souls he had met in that land, which has produced so many exalted sons of God.

He often told us, "I love all the saints. They are all my own, for in each one I see just that one Divine Beloved. But I am always loyal to my Guru. I pay homage to all who reflect the Divine; but my heart, my thoughts, never for one moment leave the blessed Guru to whom God has drawn me."

That was the wonderful experience we ourselves had when meeting these divine ones of India. It was strange: Though their personalities were so great and wonderful, through them we only felt more strongly our inner bond with Master. And the more we were in their presence, the more we felt *his* presence. I remembered Guruji telling us that God, in the ultimate sense, is the only Guru. He may use many sources to inspire you with deeper love and desire for Him; but after He has given you the channel of a true guru, then always as you approach nearer

Interior of Paramahansa Yogananda Smriti Mandir (memorial shrine) at the Ranchi YSS Ashram

4

to Him through inspiration from any source, you find that inwardly you are automatically receiving through the channel of your own guru, the one whom God has selected for you. That was what we felt — that the great inspiration and love that came to us from these saints of India was just merging us in our own blessed Master. It was such a beautiful experience.

YOGODA MATH ON THE GANGES

We arrived in Calcutta [Kolkata], * at our Yogoda Math in Dakshineswar, on July 27, 1961, which happened to be Guru Purnima day.† In India, this day is specially set aside as a time when everyone honors their own guru. Religious societies and individuals all over the country hold special *pujas,* services, and meditations, special

---

* The old spelling of the city names "Calcutta" and "Bombay" are retained throughout this narrative for historical accuracy.

† The party had entered India in Bombay [Mumbai] four days earlier.

Sri Daya Mata (center), Ananda Mata, and Mrinalini Mata arrive at Calcutta airport, 1961. Behind Daya Mataji is Sri Binayendra Dubey (later known as Swami Shyamananda). At far right is Sri Mohini Chakravarti, an official of the High Court in Calcutta, who had met and become a follower of Paramahansa Yogananda during the Guru's 1935 trip to India.

*Yogoda Math in Dakshineswar, headquarters of YSS, welcomes Sri Daya Mata and her party. **(Opposite)** Sri Daya Mata speaks in an informal satsanga with ashram residents and devotees. Mrinalini Mata is seated to the left of the altar.*

offerings of love and devotion, dedicated to their guru. So we reserved that day for Master. We had a service and meditation, and a meeting where Daya Mata spoke beautifully of our blessed Master to a gathering of about two thousand people.

VISIT TO PARAMAHANSAJI'S BOYHOOD HOME

On August 1, Sri Daya Mata conducted a YSS service at Tulsi Yogoda Ashram,* after which we were guests in the home of Master's brother, Sananda Lal Ghosh. He and his family reside in the family home at 4 Garpar Road, which Master wrote about in his *Autobiography of a Yogi.* There we had a delicious Indian meal, served on banana leaves. We visited the little attic room that Master said "had witnessed so many scenes in my turbulent *sadhana* [path of spiritual discipline]." Here our hearts fairly burst with the sacred presence of Guruji. The blessings one feels in this tiny shrine! Paramahansaji's spiritual greatness first began to manifest itself in this attic room, and a realization of his divinity overwhelmed our minds, hearts, and souls.

----

* Located on the grounds of the family home of Tulsi Narayan Bose, childhood friend and lifelong disciple of Paramahansa Yogananda. The center is adjacent to Paramahansaji's boyhood home at 4 Garpar Road.

Attic shrine in Paramahansa Yogananda's family home at 4 Garpar Road, Calcutta

You can imagine my feelings during this first pilgrimage to India! I met for the first time devotees known to me for many years through correspondence, pictures, and the stories of Guruji. I was thrilled to meet Thamu, his dear, tiny sister. How sweet and loving she is! I gathered her in my arms and shall embrace her always in my heart. I was also happy to meet another beautiful soul, Bodidi, the widow of Master's elder brother, Ananta. Master often told me about her when I was preparing his food, as one of her accomplishments is that of being an excellent cook. Whenever I prepared a curry or other Indian dish and it came out "just right," Master would say: "It is as good as Bodidi's!" Such blessed memories of our divine Gurudeva!

On July 31, Yogoda Satsanga Society held a reception for Daya Mata. It was reported in a Calcutta newspaper, which mentioned that the mayor of Calcutta had been a guest speaker: "Mr. Rajendra Nath Majumdar, Mayor of Calcutta, gave a short account of the establishment and growth of Yogoda Satsanga Society. The Mayor, like all previous speakers, paid eloquent tribute to the high spiritual attainments of Daya Mata."

(Top left) Sri Daya Mata with Purnamoyee Sarkar ("Thamu"), youngest sister of Paramahansa Yogananda. (Lower left) With "Bodidi," wife of Paramahansaji's brother Ananta Lal Ghosh, who lived with the family in the Garpar Road house (right) after her husband's early demise.

Yogoda Math in Dakshineswar, as viewed from the Ganges River

First Visit With Anandamoyi Ma

We very much wanted during this trip to India to see Anandamoyi Ma.* She travels around a good deal, without an announced itinerary, and does not stay long in one place. Sometimes devotees who want to see her have to run all over India to try to catch up with her! But strangely enough, we found that she had arrived in Calcutta just a couple of days before we did, and was staying in the large and very beautiful ashram maintained by her devotees on the banks of the Ganges not far from our YSS ashram at Dakshineswar *(photo, opposite)*. So, though we had kept Guru Purnima day just for our Master, the very next day we were able to visit her.

Wherever Anandamoyi Ma goes, as bees gather around honey, huge crowds of devotees gather around her. So there were throngs in and around her ashram that day, and special *kirtan* was going on. A large *pandal* (canopy) had been erected outdoors. At such gatherings people will sit under the *pandal*, perhaps joining in the *pujas* or *arati* or meditation; and Anandamoyi Ma will come at certain

---

* The "Bliss-Permeated Mother" (1896–1982) about whom Paramahansa Yogananda wrote in *Autobiography of a Yogi*, chapter 45. Daya Mata had met her during a previous trip to India two years earlier; this was Mrinalini Mata's first encounter with her.

times and meditate with them, or sometimes she may speak to them or inquire if anyone wants to ask a question. She is never bound by any formality. It depends on her *bhava* or mood at the time. Sometimes she doesn't even talk. She just will come and sit; and people may not say anything to her; they sit and look at her, they receive her *darshan,* and they are content. At times there will be chanting or *kirtan.* Often when she is in residence in an ashram there will be continual chanting of the name of God from morning until night, sometimes twenty-four hours a day. She has a very sweet voice when she chants, rather high, as is the singing of most Indian women; the voices of most Westerners sound heavy and gross by comparison.

When we arrived, the crowds were such that it was difficult even to get near. But when the devotees noticed Daya Mata, they greeted us very warmly. So many times they have said to us that Anandamoyi Ma has such love and regard for Daya Ma that she has told them to always treat us with the greatest respect and do everything that they can to make us comfortable. Someone told Anandamoyi Ma

Anandamoyi Ma and Daya Mata, 1961

17

that we were there, and she called us to come up to her. Everybody moved aside so we could be led through the crowd and seated right by her.

It was inexpressibly sweet to see the divine love that she has for Daya Ma. Whenever they meet, Daya Ma always just clasps Anandamoyi Ma's hands and holds them to her own face; and Anandamoyi Ma gently pats her in blessing. There is just a melting of the two. It was really so beautiful to witness.

She always speaks very lovingly and respectfully of Master, and whenever we are there she will tell everybody, "These are disciples of *Pita* Yogananda." She calls him "*Pita* (or *Pitaji*) Yogananda," which means "Father Yogananda," and expresses such love for him.[*] This always thrills us, and that is why we feel that she is one of our own.

I should describe to you Anandamoyi Ma's physical appearance. You have seen her pictures; but in person I think what you always notice most about a saint — and

_____

[*] In chapter 45 of *Autobiography of a Yogi*, where Paramahansaji describes his 1935 meeting with Anandamoyi Ma in Calcutta, he mentions that upon seeing him, the Blissful Mother joyfully exclaimed: "Father, you have come!… Father, I am meeting you for the first time in this life, after ages!"

Meeting of Anandamoyi Ma, her husband Bholanath, and Paramahansa Yogananda, Calcutta, 1935

I certainly found this with Master — is that once you look at their eyes it is hard to pay attention to much else! In Anandamoyi Ma's eyes I saw very much what I used to see in Master's — deep, deep black wells of divine love and otherworldliness. She is looking at the world, she is seeing you; but it is as if there is a little curtain there, behind which is something infinitely greater than what your physical eyes are seeing. And when she looks at you, just as when Master looked at us, it is as if she is penetrating far deeper than what is visible to the ordinary gaze. If you are not in a perfect state of consciousness, you suddenly feel very embarrassed because you know that every thought, every feeling, is revealed before these great ones. But this has a very purifying effect; and just as with Master, you do not mind. Even if you were in a mood, there was not a thought that you would mind laying open before him, because you knew that just by that gaze any wrong thought would be banished. That is the way you feel in Anandamoyi Ma's presence. Everything is seen, and you can think of nothing but Divine Mother — and of Master.

That presence of Master is what I experienced when I was in the company of the divine souls we were blessed to encounter in India. I don't know if I can

Anandamoyi Ma, photo taken at her ashram in Calcutta during Daya Mata's visit, 1961

explain it to you. You were aware of their individual personalities, of course; and you loved and revered that personality for its particular expression of Divinity. But suddenly you would find that you were not experiencing that saint before you. You were seeing his or her form, and hearing the words spoken, but what you were feeling was Master. It was as if he were saying to us, "Through these divine ones, I am showing you the India that I have loved, the India that I have always told you about, the India that can produce these great devotees of God. This is one; this is an embodiment of that Divinity." And suddenly you would so much feel Master's presence.

EARNING ONE'S SALVATION

That first day we saw Anandamoyi Ma, she was very busy since so many devotees were there, wanting her blessing and asking her questions. There was one rather cute exchange between her and a devotee. In India it is a common conception that the *darshan* (sight) of a saint is an automatic blessing — that just to see a holy person and receive a glance or touch from that saint can mean your salvation or at least the great hastening of it. And so in India you will find people who travel all over the country from one saint to another just for *darshan*. Often they don't want to meditate, they don't want to do what the saint says, they don't want to put forth any real effort to change their lives, they just want *darshan*.

So this is what one devotee that day was saying to Anandamoyi Ma: "I want your blessing, Ma, so that I can have salvation." And she replied to him: "The blessing is always there."

That did not satisfy him. "No, I want my salvation, my freedom, *now*. You can give it to me." And she said, "You have to earn it."

Well, this tussle went on and on! He just kept insisting, "No, Ma, you can give it to me, I want it now"; and she would just gently laugh or make some cute little remark back, repeatedly turning his demand aside. It was just as Master used to say: "Everybody wants you just to give God-realization to them. Nobody wants to have to work for it. But it's not so simple!"

Experiencing the Mother's Blessings

Because she didn't really have much time to give us alone on that day, she asked us to come back the next day, saying she would try to set aside some time for us. We returned the next day, a group of us, and she had us come into her little private room. She was sitting on her wooden bed, and we went and received her blessing and gave her flower garlands we had brought. Then we sat on the floor; and there may have been some conversation, but very little. Someone asked me: "What did you say to Anandamoyi Ma; what did you talk to her about?" I couldn't. I tried very hard. I thought, "This is my opportunity. I may never have it again!" But I couldn't think of one thing that I wanted to ask her; every question had been fully satisfied at the feet of Master. Anything that I might still have wanted to say to her would have been just the expression of my heart to Divine Mother — and this I knew that Anandamoyi Ma knew already.

So there was really nothing to say. When you come into the presence of a saint, you don't come seeking anything; you just want to sit there and be in that presence and absorb. That is the way we all felt. We sat for almost an hour, just

meditating in her presence. Someone in the group said afterward that while we were meditating she gazed steadily for a long time at each of us. She went from one to another, as if she were penetrating to the inner being of each one. Whether she was looking at what was within or simply sending her divine blessings, we certainly felt those blessings, and a tremendous peace.

And then her devotees came and said that she must go, that everyone was waiting for her in the *pandal*. We felt too full of that peace to go and join the crowd; we just wanted to be quiet and alone, so we went back to Yogoda Math.

Now, since this was my first trip to India, I had never seen an Indian saint other than Gurudeva; and of course I had been looking forward to meeting this saint whom Master had extolled so highly in the *Autobiography*. And while we were entranced with Anandamoyi Ma's divine love and sweetness — the wonderful elevation of consciousness that came from being in her presence — I must tell you that during that visit my mind and my sight could hardly leave Daya Ma. She went into a very deep state of meditation. I am not one who is prone to seeing lights or visions; but on this occasion there was a strong intuitive feeling of a very special presence emanating from Ma. Beginning on that first night with Ananda-moyi Ma, she went so deeply within, she was so immersed in inward communion with Divine Mother, that after each visit it took a long time before she would come back to her outer consciousness.

When we got back to the Yogoda ashram, Daya Ma was still very much in a withdrawn state. She walked out onto the balcony overlooking the Ganges (*see photo on next page*), and she sat down on the floor — someone brought an *asan* — and she went very deep into *samadhi*. She completely lost the consciousness of the body; and such presence, such divine love, was pouring out of her being. I sat down on the floor at her feet, and I wept tears. And I said to myself: "Not since we saw Gurudeva in *samadhi* have I had this experience. We speak of the saints of India, or looking forward to meeting the saints of India — oh! I have lived with one (Master), and I am living with one, who is carrying on in the same way as I felt from Gurudeva."

Inwardly I was saying to Master, "Here we have in our Daya Mata an Ananda-moyi Ma who is with us all the time. How you have blessed us!" I was feeling from her the continuation of that same love of the one Divine Mother. And I saw that whenever there is a devotee who is hungering for that love and cannot quite grasp it on his or her own, then through these channels that are so pure and so free of themselves, Divine Mother can flow. It is the same divine love no matter what channel it is flowing through; and it is such a beautiful experience to feel this. That was, you might say, my real introduction to India. From that moment on, my heart was at home in India.

In the Words of Sri Daya Mata

Excerpts from a letter to SRF monastics in America in July 1961

SRI ANANDAMOYI MA

This evening we drove to the ashram of Anandamoyi Ma, on the Ganges just a short distance from Yogoda Math....Anandamoyi Ma was out visiting some devotees at the time of our arrival, but we were glad to sit briefly on the upper porch of her ashram and to become deeply absorbed in meditation. Words are inadequate to describe the soaring of my soul during this period of communion.

After a short time, Anandamoyi Ma arrived and we were ushered into her presence. Our meeting was, once again, an unforgettable experience for me. My mind was immediately sucked within to behold the Divine Mother in all Her divine raiment, in all Her beauty, in all Her glory, in my soul, in my heart.

The state that comes upon me in the presence of Anandamoyi Ma is one that I first experienced through the blessings of my divine Guru, to whose life, to whose service, to whose thought my soul is utterly dedicated. I feel, as always, that it is he who is silently and secretly blessing me through this holy Mother.

As we took leave of her, she extended her tiny hands and again and again spoke of me as *bondhu*, "friend," to which my soul responded, "*mishti Ma, mishti Ma*," which means "sweet Mother." On the way back to our ashram my consciousness remained in that lofty state wherein no thought penetrated save this: *God alone, God alone, God alone.*

Beloved children of Master, I cannot fully describe this experience, nor have I the wish to do so. I only pray that the Divine Beloved bless each one of you with a sweeter and deeper glimpse of Her sacred presence within you. I am convinced beyond all doubt of the illimitable love She feels for each one of us. It is we who are lacking in that love for Her. Try again and again to become ever more absorbed in Her sweetness. Seek Her night and day, crying to Her, talking to Her; scolding Her when necessary with loving childishness, that She might draw closer to you, Her babe divine.

I do not know by any name what state my soul entered during this period of communion with the Beloved of my heart, but I am reminded of a few lines from Master's poem "Samadhi":

> *"From joy I came, for joy I live,*
> *In sacred joy I melt....*
> *I, in everything, enter the Great Myself.*
> *Gone forever: fitful, flickering shadows of mortal memory;*
> *Spotless is my mental sky — below, ahead, and high above;*
> *Eternity and I, one united ray.*
> *A tiny bubble of laughter, I*
> *Am become the Sea of Mirth Itself."*

These lines express better than any words of mine the joy that filled my heart, the sacred longing that permeated my being during this period of communion. By this I do not mean to imply in any way that I have entered or do enter any great and deep state such as our Gurudeva experienced in *samadhi*. I say only that a glimpse, perhaps a very small and fragmentary glimpse, of that intoxicating state was given me by our beloved Guru. I realize more than ever that every spiritual boon we receive comes by his grace; that from his gentle hand come all gifts of blessings, of joy, of love divine.

In Delhi and Banaras

After staying in Calcutta for about a week, we left for Delhi, where we spent five days. Daya Mata addressed several large gatherings in the nation's capital; at one of them she was introduced by the Chief Justice of India. Wherever she goes Daya Mata is greeted with honor, respect, and love. She receives the tributes sweetly yet impersonally, going ever deeper within. India has a way, somehow, of taking one's mind within, and Daya Mata responds to this with all her heart. Sometimes she becomes so withdrawn that we have to remind her of her waiting appointments or next engagements. When seeing people and talking of God her mind often goes so deeply within that in the middle of her conversations she will stop talking and just sit there in meditation. The spiritual atmosphere thus created is respected and appreciated in India; those who come to see Daya Mata follow her example and meditate quietly.

Satsanga *in Delhi, 1961*

In the Words of Sri Daya Mata

From a letter to SRF monastics in America

At Lahiri Mahasaya's Shrine

We sat long in the sacred shrine with its beautiful, almost life-size statue of our beloved *param-paramguru*, Lahiri Mahasaya. My mind became locked in bliss; gone was the awareness of the body and of the temple itself; only the thought of "God and I" existed. A divine and exhilarating experience came upon me — one so sacred and so dear to my heart that I am reluctant even to speak of it. I came away from that morning of meditation with my mind fully absorbed in the love of God and in the awareness of the presence of Sri Lahiri Mahasaya.

Sri Daya Mata meditating in shrine dedicated to Lahiri Mahasaya in the Banaras home of his grandson, Satya Charan Lahiri, 1961

CHAPTER II
FURTHER TRAVELS AND DIVINE FELLOWSHIP

SECOND MEETING WITH ANANDAMOYI MA

A few months later, again without any prearranged plan, our paths crossed a second time with Anandamoyi Ma's. We had been invited to the home of Sri Dubey's* daughter and her husband and their extended family in the city of Kanpur, which is between Delhi and Calcutta. Traditional families in India live together; we met the husband's mother, sister, brother, and sister-in-law. Sri Dubey himself is an exceptionally fine, spiritually minded person — you might say, the very epitome of the highest type of Master's beloved India, which includes very high ideals of family life.

---

* Sri Binayendra Narayan Dubey, who was later known by his monastic name of Swami Shyamananda Giri after he took *sannyas* initiation from Sri Daya Mata in 1970. He had met Sri Daya Mata during her first visit to India, and was appointed General Secretary of Yogoda Satsanga Society, a position he held for twelve years, until his passing in 1971.

In traditional homes, the ancient customs of family life that have come down for centuries, as Master describes in his *Autobiography*, are still practiced and taught to succeeding generations. And it was really wonderful to spend time in a number of homes in different cities where the family ideals that Master had always talked to us so much about were lived and where we could see them with our own eyes.

We were fortunate to find that Anandamoyi Ma was also staying in Kanpur at that time, at the home of one of her devotees who was the head of some large manufacturing concern. He was very well-to-do, and had a huge home and estate with very large grounds, very beautifully cared for. It was during the time of Durga Puja, the largest religious festival of the year, so the whole estate was decorated with colored lights such as are used in the West at Christmastime. Anandamoyi Ma's quarters were a little pavilion made out of canvas, a special tent the devotees had set up on the grounds — very pretty, like the dwelling of some Arabian king you might see in the movies.

*Daya Mata (**center**) and Mrinalini Mata (**fourth from left**). Visiting with the family of Swami Shyamananda (**second from left**) in Kanpur, 1961. Behind Daya Mata is Sri Banamali Das, who served as a General Secretary and member of the Board of Directors of Yogoda Satsanga Society of India.*

The first time we had seen her, in Calcutta, I had felt a bit of reserve. Our own Master was the kind of saint that people felt they could easily relate to. No matter who they were, right away they felt he was a friend or one of their own. You felt that way with Anandamoyi Ma also, but tempered with a sense of respect bordering on awe, which perhaps created a little more distance.* During our first visits with her in Calcutta, I had been remembering our relationship with Master — how beautiful, and, you might say, more personal it was because of his approachability — and I was thinking, "I wish I could feel a little more of that aspect of the Divine around Anandamoyi Ma."

Anandamoyi Ma says of herself that she is just like a drum. It doesn't do anything on its own; but it will make many different sounds depending on the way you beat it. In the same way, whatever a devotee is seeking from her, in whatever consciousness they approach her, to that she will respond. So it was that during this visit in Kanpur she satisfied completely my wish to see that more approachable side of her, that aspect of Divinity that I had wanted to see in her.

---

* Paramahansaji wrote in his *Autobiography* about Anandamoyi Ma: "The closest of dear friends, she made one feel, yet an aura of remoteness was ever around her — the paradoxical isolation of Omnipresence."

We gave her the garlands that we had brought. She had one of her devotees bring garlands, which she gave to each one of us, and she filled our hands with fruits, just laughing and being so sweet. Suddenly I no longer felt that reserve in her presence that I had felt before.

Anandamoyi Ma had just come from one of the functions being held that day, and she was only with us maybe five minutes when her devotees came and said she was expected at another *puja*. Just like the little divine child that she is, she sweetly acquiesced. You can see she has no personal wish for herself or her body, but just the thought, "However I am pleasing you all, however I am serving you all, this life belongs to you." You can feel in her that perfect resignation, and always the same even-temperedness of love and joy pouring out of her.

When I say that she is surrendered, with no personal will of her own, I don't want to give you a wrong impression. I myself had thought of her as someone completely otherworldly, not heeding the mundane details of what is happening around her. But it is quite the contrary; we were told that there is nothing that escapes her attention; she knows exactly what is going on in her organization,

and she is the one who is "running the show." The others harp to her tune. So we saw again that she was much like Master in that respect.

THE DIVINE LAUGHTER OF A SAINT

We visited her each day during our stay in Kanpur. Once when we arrived, she was in the midst of relating a story to the devotees; and she was laughing so hard that she was just rocking back and forth. We sat down and listened. This is the story she was telling:

On one of the days of Durga Puja there is a special *puja* performed for married women, during which one of the scriptures is read. This scripture is called *Chandi*, and "Chandi" is also the name used in this particular text for Divine Mother or Durga in her warlike aspect (Destroyer of Evil). At the end of this *puja*, after the priest has placed vermilion paste on the image of Durga, on her feet and her forehead, then the married women come forward and take that vermilion and place it on their own forehead. It is a special blessing from Ma Durga, which rebounds through all of their family.

Daya Mata offers garlands to Anandamoyi Ma, Calcutta, 1961.

43

So the priest was officiating before the image of Durga, and he had everything arranged just so. There was a little table holding the scripture, opened to the right page, and he was reciting from the scripture, and all the elaborate accoutrements for the *puja* had been carefully set up: the bowl of *paesh*, which is like a rice pudding, and the flowers, and the incense. It was very proper and very formal, and everything was proceeding along with great ceremony. Then he reached the part in the scripture reading where the married women are to come forward silently to take the vermilion.

Well, the poor fellow did not anticipate that the women would stampede! Everybody wanted to be the first one to get there and to be sure to get their share of the blessing. All these women, probably a hundred or more, surged forward. They toppled the priest over, and then down went the bowl of *paesh*, over went the scripture — and everything was in complete disarray!

Just as this happened Anandamoyi Ma was passing by, and in an instant she saw what was happening. So, rallying to a cause, what did she do? As she told this part, she demonstrated, dramatizing with her hands and gestures how she took action. She always wears a white cloth, like a loose robe wrapped around her. So she pulled a fold of this white cloth up over her face and came tiptoeing onto the scene. And then she suddenly spoke in a very melodramatic tone, as if she were a ghost or a spirit: "Chandi has come! CHANDI HAS COME!"

Of course, immediately all the women froze! But the priest just completely forgot himself — normally everyone is very reserved and displays the utmost respect around Anandamoyi Ma — he got up from the floor and just threw his arms around her! He no doubt felt that the spirit of Divine Mother really had come, you see. Then in the next instant, realizing what he had done, he was utterly embarrassed at his own breach of etiquette.

Relating all this to us, she couldn't stop laughing about how comical the whole thing had been. She would tell part of the story and then she would laugh — such contagious, joyous laughter — and then she would wait for one of the disciples to translate what she had said. Then she would look at us and laugh, and we would laugh, and when she saw that we had gotten that part, she would go on to the next. She has such a contagious laugh, just like Master's was. When she laughs, *everybody* laughs because they are caught up in the divine joy that just explodes out of her. Really there were times when it seemed that even her form disappeared into that joy, and I was just seeing Master sitting there — remembering how he used sometimes to relive humorous events from his life in India, and how he would laugh so hard that he couldn't get the story out.

She had sent for the priest, because she wanted us all to meet him and she wanted to laugh with him again about it. However, the word came back that he had departed already, but had remarked to one of the devotees that any amount of discomfiture he may have felt because of the stampede was more than worth it for the blessing he had received that day from Anandamoyi Ma.

So during that time in Kanpur I felt that we had seen the real Anandamoyi Ma, as I had so much wanted to see.

"I Want You to Learn From Daya Mata"

Another evening when we arrived, she was talking to a group in her private quarters. All of them were swamis. We were told afterwards that some of the most renowned swamis and spiritual teachers in India were there. All of them pay greatest homage to Anandamoyi Ma, and whenever she has a big function, some are always in attendance as speakers and so forth. We must have been there quite some time, and we were all beginning to feel that it was time to go, but we did not quite know how to gracefully get up to leave. Then Sri Dubey, who is much known in Anandamoyi Ma's ashram and very much loved by her, stood up. As soon as he did so, she burst out laughing and said in English: "Signal, signal, signal!" That was the signal for everybody to get up and go. (She knows just a few English words, which she always uses very appropriately.)

At any large gathering of her devotees when Daya Mata was present, Anandamoyi Ma always requested her to speak as well. On one of the days during Durga Puja, after the swamis had finished speaking, Daya Ma was asked to address the gathering. There were about 2,000 devotees in a huge crowd under the *pandal* (canopy). Daya Ma spoke very beautifully about Anandamoyi Ma, and about how we shouldn't just be content to have the *darshan* of such divine souls — the great love, the inspiration of God that we feel through them — but that we should actually change our lives to live according to their teachings, and try to emulate their lives. Halfway through Daya Ma's talk, Anandamoyi Ma came and sat on the dais just opposite Daya Ma, smiling sweetly in her habitual inner communion with the Infinite Mother.

I remember Anandamoyi Ma one time cited Daya Ma to the members of her ashram. Often in those large gatherings there would be a lot of commotion and talking and so on. Whenever Daya Ma and those of us who were with her came to see Anandamoyi Ma, we would sit in silence, meditating, just wanting to absorb her spiritual vibration — the bliss of her inner communion. And she used to point that out to her devotees as the example to be followed. In fact, she told some of them who had been with her for many years: "I want you to go to Daya Ma and ask her to tell you how to sit quietly and commune like that." It was a beautiful tribute to the training we had received from our own blessed Master.

THE SWEETNESS OF DIVINE FRIENDSHIP

The following day we were to leave for Calcutta. Daya Ma had spoken the night before at one of the large halls in Kanpur, and a number of people had

Daya Mata and Ananda Mata meditating at the ashram of Anandamoyi Ma

requested interviews in the morning. Anandamoyi Ma had asked us to come to see her once more, and we were going to do so after Daya Ma finished her interviews. But when the interviews were over, although we were already a little late, Daya Ma did not seem inclined to hurry. I was uneasy; but I have found that when she is going by her intuition, it is best to follow her lead, and I told myself, "Just relax, Mrinalini, everything is going to be all right." Finally she suddenly felt that now it was time to go, and so we all got in the car and drove off.

We were just about two blocks from where Anandamoyi Ma was staying when suddenly I saw her sitting in the car at the intersection we were passing. "There's Anandamoyi Ma!" I said; and as I looked back, I saw that she had seen us, and had turned completely around in her seat and was pointing to us. Both drivers slammed on the brakes, and we got out of our car and ran over to hers. There was a little conversation in Bengali, and then she said in English, "Follow, follow, follow." So we ran back, jumped in our car, and followed hers.

It was her custom when she was in any city to accept as many invitations to visit devotees' homes as her time permitted. This is a very much-coveted blessing in India, to have a saint or holy person visit, and bring that Divine Presence which blesses one's home. This morning she was going around to about five or six homes; she would go in for just a few minutes and then leave and go on to the next one. So we followed in our car, along with several other cars, on this pilgrimage to different homes of devotees.

She and Daya Ma talked a little bit while they were at the first home. Daya Ma said, "We were worried because we were late coming to your ashram; we were afraid that we were keeping you waiting." And Anandamoyi Ma replied, "But I was worried because I was late, and I didn't want to keep *you* waiting!" Then they both laughed. All had been perfectly timed, so that we would arrive at that intersection just in time to see her. Two seconds earlier or two seconds later and we would have missed her!

After a time she got up to leave. When she feels she has been in a place long enough, she just rises, and everybody else rises and that is the end of the visit, even if it is in the middle of a ceremony. She is never bound by formality. As we all made our way to the cars, someone said to Daya Ma, "Come on, she's going to your place." Of course, we did not know what he was talking about. But then

Sri Dubey's son-in-law Bhagwat, who was with us that day and whose house we were staying in, told us that he had asked Anandamoyi Ma if she would come and bless his home, too.

She had answered, "Well, I would like to, but my time is so short and my schedule is so heavy, it is absolutely impossible for me to do it this time." He had just dropped the subject, of course; and then in a few minutes she said, "Daya Mata is staying there; for her I will come." He was thrilled, and he had called his home so they would know we all were coming with Anandamoyi Ma.

So she went to his place and sat on the porch of the family home for some time. Then she got back in the car to depart. We thought that this would be the last time we would see her while we were in India, and as she drove out the driveway she kept looking back and waving to Daya Ma and saying, "*Bondhu, bondhu, bondhu, bondhu.*" *Bondhu* means "friend," and she calls Daya Ma "Daya *bondhu*" — "Daya, my friend." And Daya Ma always calls her "*mishti* Ma," which means "sweet Ma, sweet Mother." So all the way down the driveway, you could see her little hand out the window, and hear her voice saying, *"Bondhu, bondhu, bondhu"* — it was so very sweet.

Daya Mata and Swami Shyamananda saying farewell to Anandamoyi Ma

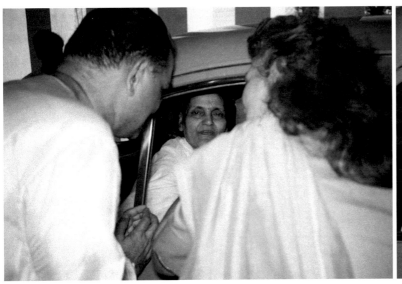

Last Meeting With Anandamoyi Ma

As it turned out, we did see her one more time before we left India. We were in Delhi, just a few weeks before our departure, and we had heard that she was in a little village maybe fifty miles from the city. So we took the opportunity to go to see her once more. She was staying in the home of another devotee, and she was more secluded there; there weren't quite so many people around.

There were four of us, and we arrived unannounced, unexpected. All we planned to do was to see her and then go right back to Delhi that same evening. But she asked us to stay. And the owners of the home were so very kind; this is typical of the hospitality of India. They immediately moved things around and fixed beds for us and prepared food, and insisted that we stay overnight.

The next day, we spent about two hours with Anandamoyi Ma, just talking with her about divine, spiritual things. She asked about the *sadhana* that we follow, and she was much interested in Master's Recharging Exercises.* Her life has

---

* The Energization Exercises, for energizing the body through conscious direction of *prana* using will power, were developed by Paramahansa Yogananda in 1916. They are taught in the *Self-Realization Fellowship Lessons*.

Traveling in Rajgir, 1961

55

been one where she has had just about every kind of spiritual experience; they have come to her naturally. And she told us how automatically during one period her body was going through something similar to what is really the basis of the Energization Exercises, the tension and relaxation, the feeling of that great life energy and the withdrawal of it into Spirit.

TOUCHING HEARTS WITH DIVINE TEACHINGS AND LOVE

The previous evening she had asked us to go with her to a meeting where several speakers were talking on spiritual subjects, and she had asked Daya Mata to speak also, as she always does at such gatherings.

Someone has asked if we used an interpreter to translate Daya Mata's words for the audiences on these occasions. We tried as much as possible to avoid interpreters for Daya Ma's talks, because she would speak for five minutes and then the interpreter would speak for fifteen! And it was obvious that he wasn't saying what Daya Mata had said. Also the spirit was lost when her words were interpreted. When it was simply Daya Ma speaking, it was a very beautiful

thing to watch. Even though some of those listening — sometimes many of them — didn't understand English, and even though they tended to be restless to begin with, when Daya Ma spoke, there would come a hush over the audience. The love for God that she radiated just had them spellbound. No matter whether they could understand what she was saying or not, there was a melting into the spirit of what she was saying; they were absorbing that spirit. It was like us with Anandamoyi Ma — many times we did not know what she was saying, but we did not mind at all. We knew enough without understanding the words, because the perception she was conveying was all going inside. We were just absorbing it like a sponge.

I remember while we were in Kanpur, Daya Ma gave a lecture one evening at the Christ Church College auditorium. Now, most Christian churches are not very much respected by the Hindus, because of misunderstandings created by overzealous missionaries. The Indian people have a tremendous love and respect for Christ; but how the missionaries usually present him in the churches, the real Hindu does not much respect. So at first I thought, "Well, this is the wrong

place to have held the meeting." But we had not made the arrangements; all such meetings were organized by local people who would then invite her to come.

To top it off, it was a rainy night — just pouring cats and dogs. When Daya Ma and I arrived at the auditorium they took us up onto a stage, and sat us in chairs that were set very neatly behind a huge conference-like table. Then a man got up and stood at the front of the stage before a microphone and introduced Daya Mata, telling a little about her, that she was from Yogoda Satsanga Society, and so forth. When he had finished, Daya Ma stood up, and I thought, "I've never before seen her stand to speak in front of a microphone." She pushed her chair back and walked toward the front of the stage, and I thought, "Sure enough, she's going to stand up before that microphone and speak." Then before I knew it, she stepped out of her shoes, and sat down on the front of the stage cross-legged. "I hope you will forgive me," she said. "I just can't speak sitting on a chair."

I had been looking at this audience when we arrived, and I had thought, "Well, this is really going to be a dud of an evening," because every one of them there looked so bored! One could sense the general feeling: "Well, I have nothing else to do, and it was raining outside, and I couldn't get home anyway. So I saw this door was open and somebody was going to speak, and so I just came in." Most of them were sitting back in their chairs, looking bored or yawning. It was almost comical to see.

But when Daya Ma walked forward and sat down on the stage, it was just as if a thunderbolt had gone through that whole auditorium. It was like a divine awakening. Everybody sat up at attention; it was as if she got up out of that chair and walked straight into their hearts. From that moment, she had that audience in the palm of her hand. I do not think there was a yawn, or a twitch — not a movement for over an hour as she talked about the eightfold path of yoga and ways to seek God. Afterward almost everyone came up to greet her personally, and many requested appointments to speak with her the following day.

Every time there was an opportunity like that for her to speak, she spoke with such force and with that great enthusiasm she had for spreading Master's teachings and making his name and his teachings of Kriya Yoga more known to his own countrymen.

In the Words of Sri Daya Mata

From Sri Daya Mata's travel diary, September 1961

YSS Ashram at Ranchi

It was nearly dusk when we arrived at Ranchi Yogoda Ashram and were ushered into the Dhyana Mandir — the place, now a shrine, where our beloved Guru had the vision that brought him to America many years ago. Here we met with the students of the YSS Vidyalaya (school).

[A few days later] we presided over a musical *satsanga* which was held in the Dhyana Mandir hall at our Ranchi Ashram, and had the opportunity to enjoy some of the most beautiful religious music that I have ever heard. I mentioned when I was

Paramahansa Yogananda Smriti Mandir, built in 1995 to replace the former Dhyana Mandir on the spot where Paramahansaji had the momentous vision that called him to America in 1920, as described in Autobiography of a Yogi, *chapter 37.*

here two years ago the visit of these devotees who have a music school (the Bihar Sangit Shiksha Bhawan) where young girls are taught to sing and to play musical instruments. Mr. and Mrs. Sen, who conduct this school, are the finest singers I have heard in all my travels in India. My mind became completely absorbed in the Eternal as these devotees chanted devotional songs to the Blessed One to whom our lives are dedicated.

Sri Daya Mata in divine ecstasy at Ranchi, 1961, during devotional chanting with Sri Sachinandan Sen and Srimati Renuka Sen (who took monastic vows after her husband's passing and was then known as Brahmacharini Mirabai)

Chapter III
In the Holy City of Puri

Swami Sri Yukteswar's Ashram

After leaving Kanpur we traveled to the ancient city of Puri, where Master's guru, Swami Sri Yukteswarji, had an ashram. The ashram is just about a block from the seaside — the Bay of Bengal. The devotees of the ashram had come to meet us, and they greeted Daya Mata with many, many garlands. Puri is one of the most spiritual of India's cities — quite populated with sadhus and *sannyasis*. And it is the custom that when the head or the leader of any religious society in India comes to Puri, the local maharaja will provide an elephant to carry the spiritual leader to their destination or their ashram. Daya Mata was accorded this honor, and me with her, as her companion.

We stayed at the Yogoda Ashram founded by Sri Yukteswarji, of course. Late that evening, I went out to the little Guru Mandir in the garden, where Sri

Yukteswarji is buried. That shrine was designed by Master as a memorial to his beloved guru; there is such a wonderful, wonderful feeling there. The minute you enter that ashram compound, immediately the mind goes to Sri Yukteswarji and you powerfully feel his divine presence there. You can easily visualize him walking along those little garden paths and standing on his little veranda looking out over the gardens. It was a very special feeling to meditate there.

(Left) Swami Sri Yukteswar, revered guru of Paramahansa Yogananda, in samadhi *meditation at his ashram in Puri (top right). He is buried in the memorial shrine shown at lower right, which was designed by Paramahansaji.*

In the Words of Sri Daya Mata

SANYAL MAHASAYA

Sri Daya Mata and her party visited this great disciple of Lahiri Mahasaya in Puri in December 1961. In a letter to SRF devotees in America, Daya Mata wrote from India: "Sanyal Mahasaya's life span, it appears, is coming to a close. We recently saw him at his ashram in Mandar Hill. He was resting. When he became aware that we were in the room he stretched forth his hand and silently blessed each one of us. Tears filled my eyes as I stood before him, realizing that this great devotee of God would soon withdraw from the body that has housed his soul for so many years. However, he has had a long and fruitful life; and surely the blessings of his beloved gurudeva, Lahiri Mahasaya, ever abide with him."*

---

* See *Autobiography of a Yogi*, chapter 35. Sanyal Mahasaya passed away about a month later, on January 18, 1962.

Sri Daya Mata and Sri Mrinalini Mata arrive at the YSS ashram atop an elephant, an honor accorded to holy personages by the Maharaja of Puri, March 1961.

About her previous visit with Sanyal Mahasaya in 1959 *(photo, opposite)*, Daya Mata wrote: "What peace one feels in the presence of these great souls whose minds have pierced the veil of *maya* — the peace sublime we have experienced in our meeting with Anandamoyi Ma, His Holiness Jagadguru Shankaracharya, Mahamahopadhyaya Pandit Gopinath Kaviraj, and now, our own Sanyal Mahasaya, one of the few living disciples of Lahiri Mahasaya.

"Here in Sanyal Mahasaya we have seen the perfect attitude of a disciple toward his guru. For him the guru is everything, he is nothing. For him, the guru is the shining light, he is but the bulb reflecting that light. For him, the guru is all wisdom; he is merely the conveyor of that wisdom, merely the spokesman for his guru. For him the guru is love and bliss divine — his eyes reflect that divinity that is his guru. His interest is not in extolling himself, the disciple, but rather in turning the spotlight of his love, understanding, and wisdom upon the inspiration of his life, Lahiri Mahasaya, that all may behold only the guru, not the disciple. How much I admire such devotees, such selfless disciples — for indeed, in the West and in the East, they are few and far between."

SRI SITARAMDAS OMKARNATH

Then the next day Daya Mata wanted to take us to meet a saint who had been living in Puri. She had seen him the last time she was in India and he was said to be 132 years old at that time. But when we inquired about him we were told that about two months earlier he had left his body. However, the person who told us that said, "There is another very famous saint staying in Puri. He has been here for about four months. Perhaps you would like to see him." Daya Mata asked who he was, and was told: "It's Sitaramdas Omkarnath." She had not heard of him before; but the moment she heard that name I remember she immediately said: "That one I want to meet." So we made arrangements to visit him that evening.

We later learned that he and Anandamoyi Ma are perhaps the two most recognized living saints in India today, the two who have the largest followings.

We went down the main road — actually just a little dirt road — near Omkarnathji's ashram. Then there was a gateway and a long pathway that winds up a little hill. On top of the hill is the ashram — a simple, perfectly plain white building. As

Sri Sitaramdas Omkarnath warmly welcomes his American guests, Puri, 1961.

we approached from a distance, we saw him coming out of an upper-story room and starting down the outside stairway. But when he saw us he turned around and waited. Later we understood that he had just been getting ready to go to his own private meditation room for meditation. But realizing that we were coming to see him, he went back to receive us, and greeted us joyously as we walked up the stairway.

Omkarnathji is about seventy,* and has a long grey beard and long matted hair coiled about his head. His body is very frail-looking, but he is full of divine vitality, and he radiates such love. Again, as with Anandamoyi Ma, it took some time before you got past the eyes — they were just filled with divine love and joy. He greeted us so warmly — especially focusing on Daya Ma — as if we had known him for years and were seeing him again after a long time of separation. Then he took us by the hand and asked the devotees to bring *asans*, little mats to sit on, and we all sat down on the little outside porch.

---

* He was born in 1892 and left his body in 1982.

For some months he had been observing *mauna*, or silence — he had not spoken a word. So to converse with us he motioned to his devotees, and they brought his little writing tablet. It was put on a small table in front of him; then for all of Ma's conversation with him, he would write on the tablet, and someone would read and someone else would translate into English. Then Ma would answer back in English, and her reply would in turn be translated for him.

Daya Mata right away perceived his devotional nature, which appealed to her as one whose approach to God has been through the path of all-consuming love. So she asked him something about the path of *bhakti*, devotion, going to God through *bhakti*. He spoke a little about that. Then we expressed interest in knowing what was the *sadhana* that he advocated for his devotees, and he began a very long discourse, explaining in detail what he recommends for his disciples as their path to God. It is centered around what they call "taking the name." That is, they will go on repeating, over and over again, a name of God. It might be "Ram, Ram, Ram, Ram" for example. And that sets up a vibration within you that attracts God, that attracts that manifestation of God.

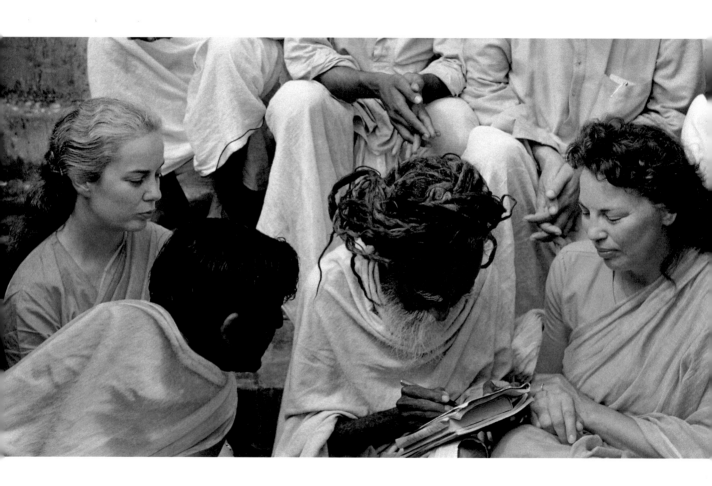

As you know, all language is vibration; and especially in the sacred Sanskrit language divine words have the power to materialize. So the name of God, when repeated, brings that vibration of God into the being of the devotee. And of course, the greater the depth of concentration that is used in the chanting, the more potent that *Japa Yoga* or mantra becomes. Omkarnathji's teaching is that as one repeats one of the names of God, and as that vibration actually begins to be felt within, then out of the vibration of the words you are repeating, the primal vibration of *Aum* begins to manifest — that first creative power, that first manifestation of God in creation. And he spoke of the different astral sounds that the *Aum* manifests in the spinal centers, heard as one's perception deepens. What he was saying was very much like the results of the *Aum* meditation technique* that Master teaches us.

---

* Taught in the *Self-Realization Fellowship Lessons*.

Under a vow of silence, Sri Sitaramdas Omkarnath converses
with Sri Daya Mata through the written word and translators.

DIVINE RELATIONSHIP BETWEEN TWO SAINTS

We were much absorbed in his deep discussion about it, which was very beautifully expressed. His whole attention was on Daya Ma; it was just between him and her. At times it was as if the rest of us hardly existed! It was so sweet to see the divine interaction between them, because he is just like a little child. Daya Ma, as we always saw when she went to a temple or into the presence of any saint, was deeply interiorized. She would be sitting there meditating; and then he would write something profound. She would hear it as it was translated, but she was just inside, absorbed. And it was very cute: he would reach over and give a little push, as if to convey, "Did you hear it?" and then he would laugh, silently, covering his mouth to preserve *mauna*. And her laughter joined in. It was so divine, so sweet.

We were there for perhaps two or three hours, absorbed in this discourse. Then it got so late, we felt we must go. "Well then, please, won't you come back tomorrow?" he asked. So we said yes, we would be very happy to come back the following day. By then, it was very dark outside, so nothing would do but that he had to take us part of the way back to our ashram.

He got up and took Daya Mata by the hand, and then he looked around and took me by the hand. We felt like little children, wrapped in divine love, as he walked us down the path all the way back to the gateway — maybe a hundred yards. And every now and then he would just gently squeeze my hand or shake my arm. It was very sweet. Without ever speaking a word, he said much. But as I said earlier, in the presence of such devotees you did not particularly want to talk. You just received from them through their divine vibration. Omkarnathji was so cheerful and sweet and childlike — and he filled you with that joy that was his own nature.

We got as far as the gateway, and Daya Ma said, "Well, now that you have walked us this far, we should take you back to your ashram." He laughed, and like a child complying with his mother's wishes, he wheeled us around and we started back up the path. We went just a few steps inside the gate, and then he indicated, "Now, that's enough." But he insisted that we could not go back to our ashram by ourselves; so he sent three of his own disciples to chaperone us.

While we were still at his ashram, as it had begun to grow dark outside, one devotee had brought in a little kerosene lamp, and by its light we had been having our divine *satsanga*. There is perfect simplicity there — only rudimentary furnishings and no electricity. If they just have a little roof over their heads, and love for God in their hearts, they are satisfied. They have no need for anything else.

So his disciples had taken lanterns from his ashram to light our way, and now we took one of them to go back to our own ashram, and another was given to the disciple that was going back with Omkarnathji. But no, he did not want that lantern. Both the lanterns had to go with us. "Oh, no. You must take one," we said. And then there was a little play fight between Daya Ma and Omkarnathji:

"No, you take it."

"No, you must take it."

This went on until finally he insisted again, pretending to be really angry, "You have to do it!" So then we took the lantern and were taken back to our ashram by the disciples, aglow with the joy and love we had received.

Sri Omkarnath accompanies Sri Daya Mata and party to the gate and back, during send-off on their first visit to his ashram, Puri, 1961.

An Exchange of Divine Ecstasy

The next morning, we went about ten or eleven, and he was waiting to greet us — if possible, even more warmly than the day before. He finished the discourse that he had started the night before. Then he asked Daya Mata something about her experience of God. So Daya Mata told him of an experience that she had had; perhaps you have heard her tell it — when her body was unwell and she was taken to the hospital for an emergency operation and almost died. She told him how she saw the beautiful great revolving light of the spiritual eye, and felt herself melting into it; and how she heard the sweet voice of Divine Mother, saying, "My child, this is death. Are you ready for it?" And Daya Mata, looking ahead into that beautiful realm opening to her gaze, answered, "Oh, yes, Mother, I'm ready!" Then the voice said, "But if I ask you to stay for Me, will you stay?" And Daya Ma said such a thrill of joy went through her that the Mother would ask her such a thing, and replied: "Of course, Mother, whatever You say."*

---

* Sri Daya Mata relates this experience in the talk "Death: Mystery Portal to a Better Land," in *Finding the Joy Within You*, published by Self-Realization Fellowship.

Omkarnathji listened with rapt attention to Daya Ma's account. And just as she was concluding the story, he wrote on his little tablet and pointed to his arm, saying, "You see? The hairs on my body are standing up in ecstasy." We looked, and we saw that the long hairs on his arm, and the hairs all over his body, were standing up. This is said to be one of the experiences of the saints, that sometimes when they are in a very high state of ecstasy, divine joy, the hairs on their body will stand up. Daya Ma later told us that she had had a secret desire, which she had never mentioned to anyone, to witness that sometime.

Then he related, "I had a very similar experience many years ago." He told us of a time when he had been close to death due to a difficulty or disease that affected his leg, and he showed us the scar on his frail leg. At that time a voice had told him, "Now is the time for you to go, but I yet have work for you to do. You must stay on a few more years, because I have divine work for you in this world."

They continued to "compare notes" back and forth about these deep and divine subjects. And with each experience that she would tell, he would just bubble with enthusiasm, as if to say, "Oh, yes, I've had that, too!" It was all so sweet and humble and simple. Then suddenly he wrote on his tablet, "It is not just chance that you have come here today. Divine Mother has brought you." He went on to write many very beautiful things about Daya Mata, such as, "Divine Mother has come to us in the forms of Durga, Saraswati, Kali Ma. And now she has come to grace our presence in the form of Daya Ma."

Then he wrote, "Today the son has found his lost mother." And with that he just threw his arms around Daya Ma, and she threw her arms around him — and the whole place was electrified with divine love and joy. I can't describe it to you!

Daya Ma said later that she felt she had known him always, that she had felt that way the moment she saw him.

One thing I very much admired was the response of the devotees around him, and this showed something of the stature of their guru. You can sometimes gauge, to a certain degree, the quality of the guru by his disciples. Around him were some of the most beautiful disciples I have seen anywhere in India. Their faces reflected that they were really in earnest in their *sadhana*, that they really spent time in meditation; and their eyes were filled with that otherworldliness that you see in the eyes of devotees who meditate deeply.

The feeling that these disciples were real devotees of God was confirmed by the way they melted into this exchange of divine love. There was no hint of jealousies or reservation, no questioning, "Now, why would my guru do that?" Many of them said that they had never seen Omkarnathji react this way to anyone. And of course with women especially, the training is always to be very much reserved. We noticed that with others who came to the ashram to see him, the disciples didn't even allow them to touch him, or to touch his feet. And yet with us, and especially with Daya Ma, he was so loving and affectionate, blessing us; and we took the dust of his feet as an expression of our great respect and reverence.

One of the main disciples, the one who did most of the translating, said again and again, "This has been the greatest day for us. We have been privileged to witness something that is seldom witnessed here on earth. We have seen here today the divine union of two divine souls. This is an experience that will remain with us always." They just could not get over this wonderful experience that had taken place.

HUMILITY: HALLMARK OF THE TRULY GREAT

Shortly after this, right in the midst of a sentence, he suddenly wrote on his little tablet, "Aren't you hungry?" We said no, we were enjoying a diviner manna. So the discussion continued a little longer, until finally he wrote, "Surely you must be hungry." We replied that we were not hungry, but that if he wanted to give us *prasad* we would be happy to receive it. *Prasad* can be anything, like fruit or a piece of candy, that is handed to you by a saint. It is considered a special blessing, and when you eat of it, you take that blessing within you.

Immediately he stood up and took us by the hand and led us over to an adjoining building, and out onto a little porch. Again he had *asans* brought for us. We were waiting for him to be seated before we sat down ourselves. But he would not sit until Daya Ma had sat, and she would not sit until he sat. Finally he laughed, just like a little child, and took our hands, and we all sat down together. Then water was brought and we started to wash our hands. No, that would not do. He got up and

The guileless simplicity of Sri Sitaramdas Omkarnath captivates Sri Daya Mata and her party, Puri, 1961.

took the water; and first he washed each of our hands with his own little hands, and then he washed the floor in front of us where the food was to be served.

I remembered Master speaking of that divine humility of the saints. And I thought, "This is an example, that the greater they become, the more little they become, the more the loving servant of all." That he would wash not only Daya Ma's hands, but mine and the others' in our party — and he did it so lovingly. Then as our food was brought he placed it in front of us. And after we were through eating, again he washed our hands for us.

I must tell you another very sweet incident. The first night when we came we brought along the camera; and while Omkarnathji was writing, one of the monks took a flash picture. Well, of course, when the light went off it surprised him, and he looked a bit startled. And then he realized that a photograph had been taken of him. In silent pantomime he play-acted with great delight. He took off his *chuddar*, and straightened up and conveyed by his expression and postures something like, "See, I'm so important — swelling with pride because my picture is being taken!" We all laughed, which delighted him. He just wanted to make you laugh, he just wanted to fill you with that divine joy and love.

After we had eaten our lunch, he presented Daya Mata with some of his books. Then it came time for us to go, and he took us by the hand and walked us all the way down the path, out the gateway and quite a way down the road. He asked Daya Mata to write, and said a few very sweet and beautiful things to Daya Ma. Then as we were ready to part, Daya Mata knelt to take the dust of his feet. He did not want her to do it, but she was there before he could prevent her. And he took the *chuddar* from off his back and put it around her shoulders. Then Daya Mata *pranamed* and backed away a few steps — she did not want to turn her back on him. Seeing this, he *pranamed* in turn, and then as we stood there *pranaming*, he backed up all the way, until he was inside the gate; and he continued backing up until he was completely out of sight. He would not turn his back on Daya Mata either. It was so very beautiful. So we had truly had a divine *satsanga* with him. That evening we returned by train to Calcutta.

In the Words of Sri Daya Mata

Excerpt from a talk to SRF monastics in 1965

SRI SITARAMDAS OMKARNATH

Having lived around a truly spiritual and a truly advanced guru such as Paramahansaji, it has been much easier for me to discriminate as to who has that realization and who does not have it. If you were to ask me what are the signs of a really great teacher, I would say that, in my mind, the first requirement would be, "Is he humble?" If I don't see that, he doesn't impress me, that's all I know. Humility is the very foundation of the spiritual path. You show me a person who is God-realized and he will first of all be a humble soul. I don't mean weak; but humble, meek. Because it is truly said, "When this 'I' shall die, then will I know who am I."

Sri Sitaramdas Omkarnath was one such divinely humble soul. When I went to see him, he rushed down the steps of his ashram to greet me, though we had never met. I was so overcome. I thought, "How kind he is! What humility! Here is a saint who is revered by millions in India, and he comes down to greet me." It humbled my own soul.

What impressed me further was that around his neck, he had tied on a string of *rudraksha* beads the slippers of his guru as a constant reminder of the disciple's devotional surrender at the guru's feet. I'm not suggesting this be done here, but in India his practice was understood. When he talked with me it was always, "What my guru said, what my guru taught." He had no thought for himself, only, "My guru said such and so." I said, "Here is someone who knows God." He was a beautiful soul.

PARAMAHANSA YOGANANDA BROUGHT THE BEST OF INDIA TO THE WORLD

My trip to India confirmed what I knew already in my heart — what all of us who were around Gurudeva Paramahansa Yogananda and have gone to India will say: You can go all over that land, or all over the world, and you can meet those who are considered to be the very greatest among Divine Mother's devotees. But truly you do not have to go one step — for our own Master brought to us the best that India has to offer; and in him you find the very highest of any incarnation that has walked this earth.

Sometimes devotees say, "Well, who impressed you most?" Or, "What was this or that one like in comparison with Master?" As Master himself said, it is not right, it is not even possible, to compare saints. With the limited instrument of the human mind, one simply cannot measure the infinity of a saint's being.

But this I can say from my own experience: It took a Yogananda, it took one of the very highest stature, with an all-rounded nature and personality such as his,

Sri Daya Mata and Sri Mrinalini Mata meditate before a shrine of Adi Shankaracharya (India's greatest exponent of Vedanta philosophy and reorganizer of the ancient monastic Swami Order), Puri, 1961.

95

to be able to come to the West, to found for the world a work such as he started, bringing the very essence of the highest and purest teachings of India, and have the West accept him. It would be very difficult for some of the other divine ones — as great as they were, as perfect as their realization was — to accomplish what Master did. Of course, they had other roles that Divine Mother assigned to them; one cannot compare and should not try to.

Among the saints in India, some manifest a predominance of *bhakti*; in others, *jnana*, or wisdom may predominate; others emphasize *karma yoga*, the path of right action; and some just roam where they feel drawn, singing the name of God. But seeing these other divine ones, we appreciated all the more how all of those qualities were blended in our own Master.

Guruji was the perfect incarnation of love. His approach to God was through *bhakti*, devotion, or *prema*, divine love. At the same time, he was a perfect *karma yogi*. From early morning until long after most of the world had gone to rest he was busily active for God. As for wisdom, there has not been a saint in India today

*Paramahansa Yogananda **(center)** with some of his disciples at SRF International Headquarters in 1947 — including Daya Mata **(left arrow)** and Mrinalini Mata **(right arrow)***

or for generations — and we have had people all over India tell us this — who has explained the depth of the scriptures as Master has. His explanations are so lucid, so simple, and his guidance is so practical. That takes real divine wisdom.

India is just crying for what Master has to give. We think of that land as the source of our own teachings and *sadhana*, and yet the vast majority there do not understand their own heritage. Just as our Guru would teach Christianity in the Christian churches, and the people would say, "Well, I never understood the real meaning of these truths before," so when Sri Daya Mata went among the Indians, speaking their own philosophy, it was just like a great light coming. Time and time again we heard the same comment: "It has taken you from the West to come to India to make us understand and appreciate our own philosophy, our own ancient culture and truth." That in itself is the most wonderful tribute to what our Master brought to us, and to what our beloved Sri Daya Mata so purely reflected as his divine representative.

The End

Paramahansa Yogananda

Paramahansa Yogananda (1893 – 1952) is widely regarded as one of the preeminent spiritual figures of our time. Born in northern India, he came to the United States in 1920, where he taught India's ancient science of meditation and the art of balanced spiritual living for more than thirty years. Through his acclaimed life story, *Autobiography of a Yogi*, and his numerous other books, Paramahansa Yogananda has introduced millions of readers to the perennial wisdom of the East. Today his spiritual and humanitarian work is carried on by Self-Realization Fellowship, the international society he founded in 1920 to disseminate his teachings worldwide.

An award-winning documentary film about Paramahansa Yogananda's life and work, *Awake: The Life of Yogananda*, was released in October 2014.

Other Books and Recordings
by Sri Mrinalini Mata

Books

Manifesting Divine Consciousness in Daily Life

The Guru-Disciple Relationship (How-to-Live Booklet)

Talks on CD

Embracing and Sharing the Universal Love of God

If You Would Know the Guru: Remembrances of Life
with Paramahansa Yogananda

Guided Meditation for Christmastime

Living in Attunement with the Divine

Look Always to the Light

The Guru: Messenger of Truth

The Interior Life

The Yoga Sadhana That Brings God's Love and Bliss

Talks on DVD

Be Messengers of God's Light and Love

In His Presence: Remembrances of Life with
Paramahansa Yogananda

Portal to the Inner Light: Official Release of
Paramahansa Yogananda's *The Second Coming of Christ:
The Resurrection of the Christ Within You*

The Second Coming of Christ: Making of a Scripture —
Reminiscences by Sri Daya Mata and Sri Mrinalini Mata

Available online at www.srfbooks.org

Books by Paramahansa Yogananda

Available at bookstores or online at www.srfbooks.org

Autobiography of a Yogi

Autobiography of a Yogi (*Audiobook, read by Sir Ben Kingsley*)

God Talks With Arjuna: The Bhagavad Gita
(A New Translation and Commentary)

The Second Coming of Christ:
The Resurrection of the Christ Within You
(A Revelatory Commentary on the Original Teachings of Jesus)

The Collected Talks and Essays
Volume I: Man's Eternal Quest
Volume II: The Divine Romance
Volume III: Journey to Self-realization

Wine of the Mystic: The Rubaiyat of Omar Khayyam—
A Spiritual Interpretation

The Yoga of Jesus

The Yoga of the Bhagavad Gita

The Science of Religion

Whispers from Eternity

Songs of the Soul

Sayings of Paramahansa Yogananda

Scientific Healing Affirmations

Where There Is Light: Insight and Inspiration for
Meeting Life's Challenges

In the Sanctuary of the Soul: A Guide to Effective Prayer

Inner Peace: How to Be Calmly Active and Actively Calm

How You Can Talk With God

Metaphysical Meditations

The Law of Success

Cosmic Chants

DVD Video
Awake: The Life of Yogananda
A film by CounterPoint Films

*A complete catalog of books and audio/video recordings —
including rare archival recordings of Paramahansa Yogananda —
is available on request or online at www.yogananda-srf.org.*

Self-Realization Fellowship Lessons

The scientific techniques of meditation taught by Paramahansa Yogananda, including Kriya Yoga — as well as his guidance on all aspects of balanced spiritual living — are presented in the *Self-Realization Fellowship Lessons*.

For further information, please ask for the free introductory booklet *Undreamed-of Possibilities*.

Self-Realization Fellowship
3880 San Rafael Avenue • Los Angeles, CA 90065-3219
Tel (323) 225-2471 • Fax (323) 225-5088

www.yogananda-srf.org